The Collected Mardles of Alec

Memories of a Life in Trimingham

Alec Reynolds

CONTENTS

Title Page
Preface
2012   1
2013   9
2014   19
2015   29
2016   38
2017   48
2018   58
2019   69
2020   79
2021   94
2022   110

Alec as a Teenager

PREFACE

Alec was born in August 1926 at The Buildings, now known as Coastguard Cottages. He had an elder sister, Daphne, and two younger brothers. Daphne and Edwin also lived most of their lives in Trimingham. Len moved to Leicester. When he was a few months old the family moved to Garden Cottage, 10 Church Street, Trimingham. When he was 4½ he went to Trimingham School, he went a few months early because Daphne would not go to school without him. When he was 5 Trimingham School closed and he then went to Overstrand School.

He left school at 14 and started work at Hall Farm, Trimingham as a farm labourer, when he was 16 he was loaned out to Beacon Farm to look after the poultry. At 18 he went back to Hall Farm, loaned out to Church Farm for ¾ months, then back to Hall Farm. At 19 he worked at Bizewell Farm Sidestrand and at 21 he worked for the WARAG for 6 months. He then got a job with Mr Duffield at Ivy Farm, Sidestrand and stayed there for 15 years. At 37 he started work for Norfolk County Council as a labourer and worked his way up to Team Leader and stayed there until he retired at 65.

When he was 35 he joined Trimingham Parish Council and made his way up to Chairman, again he resigned when he was 65.

He married Margaret, who had been a Land Girl in Trimingham, in 1946. They lived in a property on the cliff owned by Rev Page and moved into Lilac Cottage in 1956 and stayed there ever since.

Alec's "Mardles" were originally published month by month in the Trimingham Newsletter, and for the purposes of this booklet are divided into the years in which they appeared.

July 2022 Edition

2012

Frank Reynolds, Alec's Dad

Railways

Alec's father, Frank Reynolds, could remember sitting on the embankment at Trimingham as a little lad watching the men working. Alec's Grandfather had told Frank that "the spoils from the cutting was used for the embankments and that it would be loaded up into wagons and a small steam loco would give a sharp tap to send them down the line. Two men were assigned to fix a sprag to the wheels so that the wagon tipped its load. Sometimes they were a bit too over enthusiastic and the entire wagon would tip right over. Since it could not easily be righted it would be buried in the embankment." Frank said, "I suppose more than one is still there."

Moles

My Dad, Frank Reynolds, used to catch moles by traps in fields around Trimingham with his brother Percy. I can remember walking with him near Blackberry Hall and he stopped and watched a mole hill. He walked into the field and dug in his toe into the ground and flicked a mole out and killed it. He would take them home and skin them. The flesh could not be used and was buried. The skins were pegged out on a board to dry in the sun. When they were ready he put them in a Basildon Bond envelope box, as it was just the right size, and sent them by train to London where they were made into coats and hats.

George V Jubilee

Rev Buxton owned Trimingham Estate, including the houses and farms in Trimingham. In celebration of George V's Jubilee in the woodland behind Coastguard Cottages he had planted a large quantity of daffodil bulbs and had paths and seats put in so that the villagers could use the wood. There was a gate off White Gate Lane and another off the main road near Bizewell Farm. However, it was never registered as public land so after Rev Buxton's death Trimingham Estate was sold in various parcels and the wood was sold and is now private land.

Battle Area

The low ground which is down White Post Lane (next to the Council Houses) was the Battle Area during the Second World War. Soldiers used it during the week for manoeuvres, and the Home Guard at weekends. There was a Churchill Tank on the cliff top, besides a Plantation called "The Borres", which is no longer there. The tank was used for target practice. The farm labourers from Hick's Farm were harvesting the sugar beet one autumn when they suddenly had shots fired over their heads from the soldiers practising. The soldiers were supposed to have a man with a red flag, one from Bizewell Farm end and one from the Council Houses end, but they did not do that that day. Labourers did not stay very long. When rolling the battle field with a tractor there would be small explosions from the phosphorous from the grenades.

Team men

My father Frank and Arthur Hunt were Team Men at Hall Farm, for Mr Harrison. Team Men had to get up early in the morning, about 5.00am, to clean out the stable, feed the horses, and groom them so that they were ready for the day's work. After the day's work they would feed them with hay, oats, chafe and mangold. They would give them a clean bed of straw for them to lie down for the night. When the tractor took over they just had about 4 horses and one Team Man, who was Mr Hunt. Father Frank was the Tractor driver; it was the first one in Trimingham and was an International W30, which did the ploughing and working the land.

The Tale of Straw

When I first started work on a farm the straw was cut with a Binder (1), and then set in shocks to ripen off (2). It was then pitched onto a wagon (3), from there it was made into a stack (4). The stack was thatched with wheat and straw (5) to keep the rain out. It was then thrashed to take the corn out (6). The straw was again stacked (7). It was then loaded onto a wagon (8) and unloaded (9) for bedding down cattle. The soiled straw was cleared out (10) and loaded onto a cart (11), which was pulled by horse, unloaded (12) and made into a muck heap to rot away. Finally it was picked up again (13) and spread (14) onto the land, as manure, for the next crop of straw.

Sugar Beet

Sugar beet were drilled on land that had been well cultivated. It was drilled in rows of 18ins or 20ins apart. It was drilled very thick to make sure of a crop. After the beet plants were big enough to see they were horse-hoed. After that the farm workers would go into the field with hoes to thin out the beet, leaving about 7/8ins between each plant. This would be done from the second week in May until the end of July. The fields had to be hoed by hand twice. Each man then had their own acre to hoe, and was paid so much an acre. From September to January the beet would be dug out of the ground by a fork or a digger by hand. They would be laid four rows in one; they were then topped by a hook. The beet would be put in heaps in the field; the tops (or leaves) were left in the rows. The beet were then carted off the land, some were taken into the Railway Yard and loaded onto trucks, some were put into a pile on the roadside and then loaded onto lorries. The entire beet crop ended up at Cantley Sugar Beet Factory. The beet tops were fed to the cattle, nothing was wasted. All the loading and unloading was done by manual labour.

Rev Buxton

In the early 1900s most of the houses and all the farms in Trimingham belonged to the Buxton family. John Henry passed the estate to Rev Arthur Buxton, and I can remember him as my landlord. When the Rev Buxton died Margaret and I were given the opportunity to purchase our house, which we did. Rev Buxton had a gamekeeper who lived in Keeper's Cottage; Woodlands' Club House now stands on that site. There was also a Shooting Lodge in the woods at Woodlands. When in North Norfolk the Rev Buxton lived at Upton House, which is the house opposite the traffic lights at the junction of Overstrand Road / Norwich Road at Cromer. Rev Buxton was the Rector at All Souls, Langham Place, London, next to the BBC.

<u>Bonnyrigg and Cliff House</u>

The property owned by June and Patrick Carpmael used to be known as Bonnyrigg. Before the Second World War; it was owned by Jack Hulbert, Cecily Courtneidge and Peter Haddon. They used to come and stay there in the summer months. They were well known actors of their time. To the sea-side of the house was a lovely hard-court Tennis Court. Cliff House was once owned by Major Pickford and his wife. He was a Headmaster at Paston Grammar School and he gave the lions on the gateposts at the entrance of the school on Grammar School Road.

Christmas at Alice's

I remember Christmas as a boy, which was a lot of years ago. In our house Christmas started on Christmas Eve. After us children had gone to bed Mum and Dad decorated the tree and put up all the trimmings. When we got up on Christmas morning it looked lovely with the gifts around the tree. Also on Christmas Eve Mum would do all the baking and get the dinner prepared. Next to Alice's shop was a Tea Rooms, which was also run by the Pearson family, and in the Tea Rooms they sold Christmas gifts and it was great to go in and walk round and look at all toys etc for sale. In the school we had a fancy dress day, a present from the Christmas tree, played games and had a good meal. It was nice to walk down the street and see the candles alight on the trees. What memories, they were the good days.

2013

Alec with his Trimingham Pilgrims Football Shirt

Early Years

When I was a young lad, which was a long time ago, I started school at Trimingham when I was 4½ years old. The only reason I started then was because my sister would not go to school unless I went, so I never had much choice. When I was

5 Trimingham School closed and we then went to Overstrand School. At that time of day you went to a school until you were old enough to leave. The only chance of changing to a Grammar School was if your birthday came at the right time and you could sit an entrance examination, or if your parents could afford it.

We went to Overstrand by Green & Grey Coaches, which belonged to Mr Babbage of Cromer. If he was busy on Day Trips he would send out Maroon Coaches of Overstrand, which belonged to Mr Reynolds, but he was not a relation of mine. On Mondays we went to carpentry lessons at Cromer, we had to walk to Cromer from Overstrand. At dinner time we had 1½ hours, we had to sit in the classroom for ½ hour and have our meal. After that we would go for a walk down on the beach and then to the classroom. For dinner we took a large potato and baked it near the open coal fire, also we had a bottle of milk which was also warmed up. The good old days. The infants had a room of their own. The big room was divided with a curtain; one side was classes 2, 3, and 4 and the other side classes 5, 6, and 7.

14th February – Valentine's Day

As a lad in the village we used to look forward to Valentine. We used to go around to relations and knock on the door. We would leave a small present and run away. After that we would wrap up a parcel of old papers in brown paper, tie it up with string, leaving a long piece of string attached to the parcel. We would knock on the door and when the door was opened and we would pull the parcel away and run away. I expect they would have an idea who we were. It was just a bit of harmless fun.

Football

Trimingham had a football team called "Trimingham Pilgrims" and their colours were amber and black shirts with black shorts, they wore hobnail boots. They used to work in the morning, go home and have their dinner and then play football. The football pitch was on the cliff near where the Pottery is now. The goal posts and nets were kept in the loft of the Pilgrim Shelter. On a Saturday, at dinner time, Uncle Bert Gray used to put the posts and nets up and mark out the pitch. Some of the players were Joe and Haward Kidd, Frank Reynolds, Reggie Neave from Overstrand and Harold Rounce. Harold always played on the wing, he was a stocky fellow and on the pitch there was a "pit" hole, which filled with water when it rained and Harold always fell in it. The trouble with playing on the cliff top, when the wind was blowing hard off the land, the players spent a good bit of time going on the beach to get the ball back. Everyone enjoyed the games, which the Pilgrims mostly lost. I can remember as a lad I used to get to the away matches in a sidecar as one of the players had a motorbike.

Dances

We used to have dances in the school. Dances were very popular in the surrounding villages. In my younger days we used to go to other village halls to dances. They would support ours, villages used to mix together in those days. We used to do all the old dances. One I remember was a Spot Dance. One of the Committee Members who ran the dance would pick a spot on the floor. The music would stop and the couple who were on that spot would get a prize. In later years we did Scottish dancing, someone came to give us lessons, but we never wore a kilt.

Whist Drives

We used to have Whist Drives in the School as this was used as the Village Hall after the school was closed. People used to come from the villages all around us. It was very popular and the hall got very full and sometimes the other rooms of the school had to be used so that everyone could play. At Christmas time people hoped to win their Christmas Dinner, the prizes were poultry, rabbits etc. There was no trouble parking as people either walked or came on their bicycles. When Rev Buxton who owned the school died, he left it to the village.

Coal Mining

A Company came and drilled for coal at Gimingham, near Grove Farm on the Gimingham/Trimingham borders. It was one of the worst winters, everywhere was covered with snow and ice whilst they were drilling. They did find coal, how much I don't know, but they know where it is – if they will ever come back we do not know. The big machinery had a job to get about because of the bad weather.

Farm Work

When I started working on a farm in 1940 I was thirteen. It was all horse work, most of the ploughing would be done October to February. The crops were mostly oats, barley, wheat, sugar beet, mangolds and fetches which were feed for the cattle. Wheat was drilled in December, the other crops in the spring, mangold was the last crop to be drilled in April. The land was worked both ways before the drill went into the field. The fields were much smaller then with hedges all around them. They were all cut by hand with a reef hook, the cuttings were used for stack bottom or the mangold hales. Sugar beet was cut out seven inches apart by hand, starting the second week of May to July. Then harvest would start, the corn was cut with a binder. Before starting we would mow around the headline with a scythe about six feet wide to make room for the binder to work. It would throw sheaves out which were tied up with string, and then they were set up in row to ripen out. After a few days they were put into stacks. The threshing machine then came and threshed the corn out which was put into sacks. The weights were: Oats 12 stone, Barley 14 stone, Wheat 18 Stone. The sacks all had to be manhandled. The weights listed were when they had been weighed, before that they would have been much heavier. After harvest the stacks would stand for a while, and would then get thatched to keep them dry. The next operation would be to riffle the stubble ready for ploughing. It was then the turn of the sugar beet; these were all dug and topped by hand. This work would last from the end of September to the end of December. There were no waterproofs in those days; you had sacks tied around your legs, waist and shoulders. You had to work in all weathers, if not you did not get paid.

Trade in Trimingham

In the village we had two shops and you could get everything from them, without going out of the village. There was also a coal yard run by Plumbley, in the Station Yard. Tradesmen also delivered in the village:

From Mundesley – Burton's Bakers, Gedge Baker, Rusts Groceries and International Stores, Moys (for coal), Mr Briggs for accumulators for radios (on an exchange basis: you took one in one week and Mr Briggs charged it and you collected it the next week). The butchers were Frostdick, and Twig the Milkman;

From Trunch – Mr Pike for groceries and paraffin, Mr Puncher, greengrocer;

From Southrepps – Mr Bird, the butcher, Mr Drury, the baker;

From Cromer – Rusts, International Stores, Mutimores – all were grocers, Bird, Gibbons, Russell – all were butchers;

From North Walsham – Old Bear Stores, grocers, Blyths, ironmongers and garden tools, Mr Bloom, butcher. Mr Bloom got stuck in the snow at Keepers Loke and my Dad, Frank, got him out and he put his van in the barn at Hall Farm and caught the train back to North Walsham.

All these tradesmen came through Trimingham, there only half the number houses then, and they delivered to your house. They served the other villages around as well.

Pilgrim Shelter

I was reading that it would be lost to the sea within 20 years. I have been retired for 22 years; there had been very little cliff erosion behind the Shelter in those years. If the ground is not cultivated it will stand another 50 years. When it was built it had a small coal fire and old windows which were draughty and in the winter it was cold in there. Now it has got double glazing and electric heating, which makes it very warm. I also read about putting a kitchen and toilets in the Church – I am a great believer in that, but it is not far from Pilgrim Shelter.

Boys Brigade

I saw a picture in the EDP about the Boys Brigade from Norwich coming to Trimingham. Yes, they did. They used to arrive at Trimingham Station about 10.30am on a Saturday. They would play their musical instruments from the Station as they walked through the village to the Education Hut down Gimingham Hill. It was always August Bank Holiday week when they came, they stayed for two weeks. They would play the music from the Education Hut back to Trimingham Station where they would catch the train back to Norwich, also on a Saturday. During their stay you could hear the music in the background.

Vehicles in the Village

In the village as a lad there were not many motor vehicles. The ones I can remember were:

<u>Mr Harrison</u> – one car,
<u>The Rectory</u> – one car,
<u>The Coal yard</u> – one car,
<u>Mr Pearson</u> – two Austins,
<u>Rev Page</u> – one Hillman and one Rover,
<u>Mr Barclay</u> – one Austin,
<u>Mr Clark, Fishmonger</u> – one Ford van,
<u>Mr Bullimore</u> – one Royal Enfield Motorbike
<u>Mr Knights</u> – one Matchless Motorbike.

Compare that with the motor cars in the village today. I think every house had a bicycle and at that time we used to play ball in the Street, how time has changed.

2014

Margaret in Land Army Uniform

WOMEN'S LAND ARMY (ENGLAND AND WALES).
RELEASE CERTIFICATE.

The Women's Land Army for England and Wales acknowledges with appreciation the services given by

Miss Margaret Thompson

who has been an enrolled member for the period from

24 . 7 . 1943 to   23 . 7 . 1946

and has this day been granted a willing release.

Margaret's De-Mob Certificate

Date 13th July 1946

COUNTY SECRETARY, WOMEN'S LAND ARMY.

Farm Animals in the Village

The following kept animals:

<u>Beacon Farm</u> – Horses, Bullocks, Poultry
<u>Church Farm</u> – Horses, Bullocks, Cows, Poultry
<u>Hall Farm</u> – Horses, Cows, Bullocks, Pigs, Poultry
<u>Blackberry Hall</u> – Bullocks, Pigs and a Donkey

Now most of the farm buildings have been turned into living accommodation. All the above farmers had to grow hay to feed the animals in the winter. The seed was set in April and the hay was cut and stacked in June the following year.

Gardening

My vegetable garden was a great success in 2013, apart from those eaten by the Cabbage White Butterflies. The lettuces, radishes, carrots, beetroots and broad beans did very well. The potatoes were very slow coming up, but they did eventually, and they were good. I set a row of garden peas and I noticed that they kept getting thicker and thicker and I realised that the Sweet Pears had taken over and there was not an eating pea to be seen. I know what happened: I burnt the rubbish, which included the Sweet Peas which lay on the ground. I dug the ground deeper and it must have brought the seed to the top and they also struck so I ended up with a self-sown row and the row I had set of Sweet Peas and they made a marvellous show. I have been burning garden rubbish on that same area for years. The amount of seed that came up would have cost pounds

Letter to the Newspaper: What a kind Gentleman!

Dear Sirs,

On 26th January a friend and I had our lunch at The Swan Public House in Stalham. The food was well cooked and served with very friendly staff. When we came out, it was pouring with rain. As I am disabled and walk with two sticks my friend went and unlocked the car for me. As I started walking to the car a gentleman came walking down the car park towards me with his shopping and an umbrella. When he got near to me, he stopped and put the umbrella over me and walked me to my car. What a kind thought and I hope he will read this letter so that I can thank him very much for his kindness. There are still some good people around.

Yours faithfully, Mr A Reynolds

Chapel Folk

The Methodist Chapel, which was in Middle Street, was well attended. Before the war, in summer time Sidestrand Hall was a holiday place – I think for people who were recovering from not being well. They used to walk along the cliff footpath to the Chapel for the Sunday service. The cliff top was crowded with people. After the Chapel was closed it was used by St John's Ambulance. The Station Master from Trimingham, William Secker, took the classes in First Aid. My brother, Len, had a lot of interest in this and he ended up doing that sort of work.

Sea Scouts

Trimingham had a Sea Scouts Troop and we used to meet in the School. In the front of the School we had a huge flag pole on which we flew the flag on different occasions. We used to go to camp at weekend and one place was on the cliff top in The Plantation, which is no longer there. We also went to Blickling Hall, and there were hundreds of Sea Scouts there, we all had boats on the lake. Trimingham won the Best Camp, and we got a

Shield. One year there was a group of Scouts camping in the area from Barnsley and they took us, the Sea Scouts, to Yarmouth for the day. We took over the lakes on the front. I think the residents of Yarmouth thought that the Armada had arrived.

Clearing the Mines

During the War the cliffs between Mundesley and Sidestrand were mined, the mines were laid just over the cliff edge to the bottom. We could not get onto the beach for several years. There was a barbed wire barrier Mundesley end and Sidestrand end, also along the top of the cliffs to say "Keep Out Mines". It took several years to clear the mines after the war as the cliffs had fallen and the mines had moved. It was a dangerous task to clear them as our cliffs were the most dangerous ones to tackle. Several people got blown up, civilians and armed forces.

Wartime Routines

During Wartime in Trimingham there was Home Guard, and ARP, which later became Civil Defence. Also in the summer when the corn was getting ripe we had to do Fire Watch. When on duty for Fire Watch we had walk around checking everything was alright, we started at 9.00pm and finished at 5.00am, then got ready for work. We also had a Searchlight and Anti aircraft guns at the top of Church Lane on the right-hand side. The Home Guard patrolled the cliffs. Pilgrim Shelter was their Headquarters. The Civil Defence made Pilgrim Shelter ready if needed.

Milking

Margaret, who was my wife for 59 years, had to join the Forces or the Land Army, and she chose the Land Army. She did so long at Agricultural College. She was sent to Trimingham to work at Hall Farm, the foreman was Mr Chris Harrison. She milked the cows. One morning she was trying to get the cows in the milking parlour, it was pitch black, you were not allowed a light. Anyhow she got them all in but one. The one she could not get in was the neighbouring Farmer's bull which had broken away from its own herd. Margaret never did live it down. Another time the head cowman went down the Southrepps Road to Mill Pease to bring the cows in for milking, he thought he saw someone on the field. He left the cows and ran back to the farm and told Margaret she would have to go and fetch the cows, which she did. Why he did not open the gate… The cows would have walked home on their own! The cows all had to be milked, the milk cooled, labelled how much was in each churn and out ready for the lorry to pick up at 8.00am so that it could be loaded onto the Norwich train.

Rabbiting

During the winter months on a Saturday afternoon and Sunday morning my Dad, his Brother and I as a young lad went rabbiting around the farm hedges and railway banks (during the Spring the rabbits would be breeding and would be no good for eating). We used to set out with the ferrets, long-handle spades, which was the proper spade for the job, and purse nets which were about two foot square (Dad used to make them with string). When we got to our destination we would look to see how many rabbit burrows and find the main one. We put the ferret down it on a long line or sometimes we put a bit of string around its mouth and head. After the ferret was put down the burrow you would put the nets over the other burrows and if the rabbits tried to escape they would get tangled in the nets. If they did not appear then you would start digging, sometimes for hours, but another time you would be lucky and find the rabbits straight away. After all that you would bring the rabbits home and hang them up in the shed. During the week Mother would skin them and cook them. What a great meal and what a lovely smell when they were cooking. The skins would sell for about two old pence each.

Home Guards

During the Second World War we had soldiers billeted at Greystones, which was then called Bar Haven (previous to that it was called The White House). Also there were Wrens billeted in High Lawns, they had a tall wooden building on the cliffs behind Beacon Farm. It was an octagonal shape and it was used as a look-out for shipping. The Home Guard were on duty at night and soldiers during the day. It was a firm from Norwich which built the building used by the Wrens. They kept the wood and all their tools in the Cart Shed behind the barn at

Beacon Farm, at that time I was working at Beacon Farm. The soldiers were also used to guard at the Beacon Hill which was used by Air Force.

Evacuees

They came from Dagenham and arrived in Trimingham at the School. They went to the different homes where they stayed for a long while. It made a difference to the local children going to school. We went one week in the morning and the next week in the afternoon. Eventually they opened Trimingham School and also Sidestrand Hall and we got back to normal schooling. At Christmas the Evacuees gave us a party which was at the hall down the Londs at Overstrand. We all got a present but they got my name wrong, instead of being Alec they had my name as Alice so I ended up with a knitting bag. It took a long while to live it down, but the thought was there.

Aeroplanes

During the Second World War and after there used to be aeroplanes flying along the coast. Sometimes they would tow a target which was fitted to a steel wire rope; it was well away from the plane. The plane would be flying peacefully along the coast and then the planes came over and they started practice-shooting at the target and it would go on practically most of the day. Before the Second World War small aeroplanes would go by with advertising banners trailing behind them, and I can remember one for Ovaltine. During the war there were hundreds of Bombers and Fighter Planes filling the skies heading towards Germany for bombing.

2015

Alec with a Grey Fergie

Oranges

It was December 21st 1948 and Trimingham beach was covered with oranges. As all along the coast our cliffs were mined we had to go to Mundesley or Sidestrand and walk to Trimingham, being very careful. The ship ran aground on Haisbro Sands, and was called SS Bosphorus, she had to discharge the load to be towed off the sands. I think it was heading to Norway for the Christmas Market. At Sidestrand there was a man who had a rope from the cliff to the beach, one man tied the rope to the orange boxes and there were men on the cliff hauling them up. I had two brothers Len and Edwin and they walked to Mundesley and they got a few oranges. When they got to the top of the cliff the Policeman took them away from them and told them they belonged to the Customs. I expect he had them for Christmas, so Mum and Dad never had any.

Trimingham Sea Scouts

Before the War we used to meet in the School where we learnt semaphore and Morse code. On a Sunday morning we used to go to Cromer Coastguard Station where we had a dinghy and canoe, kept on the beach. Once when we were in the canoe one of the boys got very wet so he took his shirt off and laid it on the rocks, and he collected some wood and lit a fire to dry it. In the meantime we went back out to sea in the canoe. A man from the village came along the beach, collected a lot of wood and put it on the fire we had lit. When we came ashore Ronnie was looking for his shirt and all he found were the buttons, the rest had got burnt up.

Life on the Farm

When I left school I started work at the farm and got sixteen shillings a week, out of this I had to pay for 2 stamps, Employment and National Health. For that money I worked 52 hours a week in the summer and 48 hours a week in the winter. Out of that wage I had to buy the tools I used including a Muck fork, a Reef Hook, a Sugar Reef Hook and Digger, and a Digging Spade. The Fork was for cleaning out the Cattle Sheds, the Sugar Beet was for topping the Beet, and the Digger was for digging the Sugar Beet up. The spade was for digging the drains; the Reef Hook was for cutting the hedges. It was all manual work, no machines at that time. The first pair of leather boots I bought for work cost sixteen shillings.

Local Enterprise

Mr & Mrs Lamb lived in Greystones which was called Bar Haven. They took in visitors and sold ice creams and minerals. They had a small golf course in their grounds. The grounds also included the land where the current bungalows are. The main road was not there, it was just the old Coast Road. Mr Lamb was going to build bungalows where the main road is, it was all fields then. He built one which he never got finished. My Dad and some other men started to dig the road near the Church and the bungalow on the left, which always looks nice with a well kept garden. The reason the bungalow never got finished was because the war started and Mr Lamb went away to serve in the war and never returned. The bungalow was finished after the war. It was used by the Army during the war.

Land the Cliff Side of the Road

From Pilgrim Shelter to Sidestrand Church there were five Plantations and 23 fields, some small and others bigger. All the fields had hedges, banks and trees. Some fields on the low ground were wet so they had ditches around them which drained a lot of water which went under the road and drained away. Now there are about 5 fields. Years ago a lot of land had drain pipes which ran to the cliffs. Most of these pipes got ploughed out when deep ploughing was done by tractor. Think of all the water which the trees and hedges soaked up. I know with the big machinery which is used on the farms today is why there are the big fields. There are not any hedges to cut or drains to dig now which took several men weeks to do. All the fields mentioned I have worked on most of them.

Water Supplies

When Trimingham first got water in the village there was a big tank that stood high on a big metal frame. The water supplied the houses for the first time and it was great not to have to carry pails of water for drinking and cooking. For washing clothes we used soft water from a tank which collected it from the roof of the house. Some people had a pump/well. Before the water came to the village we all went to the Village Pump which was fed from the spring. The Tank was at the top of Middle Street. People from the top end such as Middle Street and as far as Beacon Hill got their water from the Pump opposite the Crown & Anchor; and Church Street got their water from a pump at the top of my garden.

Farming and Fishing

Each Farm kept cows, and some of the milk they delivered around the village. A lady from Church Farm delivered by bicycle, she had gallon cans on her handlebars and she would go up to the door and asked how much they wanted. She would then ladle out of the cans into the customer's jug. Another Farmer did the same, but he had a pony and trap. No Health checks then. We had several fishermen in the village. In those days they used to carry the boats onto the beach for the season and then bring them back up the cliffs for the winter. They would paint them for the next season. When you think those boats were made of wood and iron, a lot of weight to carry up and down the cliffs.

Tractors

Father Frank was the first tractor driver in the village. He worked for Mr Chris Harrison of Hall Farm. Mr Harrison bought an International W30 and it took over from the horses such as ploughing and cultivating. At that time of day the tractor had all iron wheels with spuds on the back wheels to grip. Dad was ploughing on the low ground; it had a wet patch into which the tractor sank. The more he tried to get out the further he sank. Dad had to leave the tractor stuck all night. The next day a bus driver brought some heavy jacks and wood and eventually the tractor came out and Dad started to do the ploughing again; that was the pleasure of tractor driving.

Travel

We used to play in the street; there were only 5 cars in the village. We had a good railway: to Cromer one way and the other way to North Walsham and Norwich. It was a lovely way to travel, look around the shops and come home. Also by rail the milk from the farms would be in 17 gallon churns and go to the Milk Marketing Board in Norwich. It was a lot of weight to carry down the steps onto the platform and on to the train. We also had a coal yard which delivered coal around the villages. Also by rail a lot of the cattle would go to Norwich Market. In those days we had a school, a hotel, and a chapel which were well attended. We also had a fish monger who went around delivering the fish which he got off the train which came from Yarmouth and Lowestoft. He smoked his own herring.

Bulls

I worked on a dairy farm at Sidestrand and we had a great herd of cows. We had three bulls on the field; they all had a ring in the nose and a mask over the face. I was left on the farm on my own looking after everything. There were builders working in the farmhouse while the farmer was on holiday. One day one of the bulls lost its mask, so I asked one of the builders if I caught the bull would he help me. He said, "No way will I come on the field where the bulls are." So I asked if he would stand behind the hedge, which he did. I managed to catch the bull and he handed the mask through the hedge and I got it put back on and I got back off the field safe.

Barbers

As a child I never went to a hairdresser, a local man used to cut it, my Uncle who lived opposite to the Church. Others were Icky Riseborough at Sidestrand, Arthur Amiss who lived near the old Crown & Anchor. Later we used to go to the Crown & Anchor and have a hair-cut. Then it was to the Pilgrim Shelter and it was cut by Billy Dunham who came from Southrepps. When he stopped Leonard Bennett, also from Southrepps, took over and he came to the house. Now Julie from the School House, just across the road from me, comes and does it and I have to pay so much for a search fee!

Highway Maintenance

Before I got the lorry I was in construction gangs of about 20 men. The work involved widening the roads and making new footpaths. In the winter the work was gritting icy roads which meant getting up at 3.30am and continuing until the roads were all gritted. Sometimes it meant that we worked very long hours, not getting home for over 12/15 hours. Before I worked for Norfolk County Council I worked at Ivy Farm, Sidestrand and one of the winter jobs I did was gritting but it was then with a tractor and trailer. I would drive the tractor and a man from the Council would stand on the trailer and spread the sand or salt on the road. He had the warmest job as the tractor I drove had no cab.

2016

Alec's Dad Frank

Alec with his Second Car, a Ford Popular

More Bulls

One morning when I went to work on the farm they said to me, you are in the cow-house today helping the Vet as all the cows are being dehorned, i.e. having their horns removed. The first thing to be done was put a clove-hitch on top of the cow's head, it was a tourniquet to stop the blood. The Vet then injected the head to numb it, he would test to make sure it was numb, and then we used a hack saw and sawed the horns off, not a nice job. Nowadays the calves' horns are done when they are a few days old, they are burnt off with caustic soda.

Home Economics

As you drive up and down The Street, look at the gardens, they are all grass and flower-beds. Years ago they would be all full of vegetables for the family to live on. There were not many lawn-mowers in the village then. At the top of the garden several houses kept pigs, poultry and rabbits. Some had a pig killed for their own use, eggs were for the table and to bake with. The rabbits were sold for extra money, they were tame ones. In the winter my Dad, Uncle and I on a Saturday afternoon or Sunday morning went rabbiting with the ferrets around the farms. We ate some, which was a good meal; the others were sold to villagers for one old penny each.

Horses and Tractors

When I started work at Hall Farm for Mr Harrison, it was horses. My Dad drove the tractor. We used to go in the field at 7.30am until 4.30pm, a long day, walking up and down the fields. When the sugar beet started, Dad drove a standard Ford tractor which carted the beet into Station Yard. Dad let me drive on the field, I was fourteen years old. Later in life I drove Fordson, Fordson Major, David Brown, and Nuffield Ferguson. The first one was all petrol, and then started on petrol and when it got warm you switched over to oil. Then it was all diesel, which it still is. I done the ploughing, cultivation, drilling, anything that was to be done on the land, also driving a combine.

Mines!

During the War the cliffs were mined between Sidestrand and Mundesley. There was a barbed wire barrier across the beach at both ends and along the cliff top and another one about 50 yards inland from the cliff top. There were signs all the way along it saying "DANGER MINES KEEP OUT". The beach had no access for several years. The land-mines came in twos bolted together for transport. They were stored on top of the cliff behind Pilgrim Shelter. The Royal Engineers took them apart and put them in the cliffs, they put the detonators in them, they wired in a phase of 8. It was a terrific bang when they exploded. This done a lot of harm to the cliff and also to some properties. When they tried to clear them they tried washing them out, they had big generators on the beach pumping thousands of gallons of sea water into the cliffs, but this was not successful so at the end they used mine detectors.

Poultry

Christmas 2015 brought back a lot of memories about poultry. We used to buy day-old cockerels. We would put a hurricane lamp in the hut, and they cuddled around it for warmth. Then at Christmas time they would be ready to be prepared for the table. My brother-in-law and I would start plucking about a fortnight before Christmas and my wife would draw them ready for the oven. They were long days as we would leave off from work, have our tea and work until midnight. We were glad when it was all finished and we hoped for a cold spell so they kept well.

My Cars

Up until 2015 I always enjoyed driving my various cars and towing my caravans (approximately 40 years) mainly to Scotland. Now enjoy being chauffeured about and looking at the countryside as we travel along.

The cars I have owned were:

Standard 12 (1934 Black); Morris 8 (1936 Blue); Vauxhall 12 (1936 Grey); Ford Poplar 8 (1961 Fawn); Ford Anglia 960 (1963 Blue); V. Beetle 1200 (1970 White); Maxi 1700 (Green); Escort 1300 (Red); Allegro 1300 (White); Ford Cortinas (Blue, Bronze, Two-Tone Green & Red); 6 Volvos (2 Red, Maroon, 3 Blue); 2 Citroens (Grey, Mediterranean Blue); 1 Peugeot (Black).

Caravans were:
Sprite Cadet, Monza, Ace Diplomat, Fleetwood, Thompson, Cornish and 4 Edliss.

Pilgrim Shelter 2

Pilgrim Shelter has served the Village well. At first it was a Men's Club, and then a lady lived in part of it for 2 years. It was a Post Office and also used as a Doctor's Surgery. Now it is made full use of with activities. When it was just a Men's Club all the social events were held in old School. When Pilgrim Shelter was built all the traffic went passed it, then the new road was made. The old road was then quiet and good to take the dog for a walk. I can remember the day it was opened and it has served Trimingham well.

Water Supply

I think the water supply came into the village late 1950. Before that we went to the village pump to get our drinking water. You did not waste it then as some of the pumps were a good distance to walk and carry the water home. The water for washing came from a pump in the garden or water butts. The water butts were filled with rain from the roof of the premises. Before it went into the water butts there was an old sock tied to the spout of the water trough to stop the dirt from going into the butt, also there was the same thing on the water pump. If you got a dry time the wells in the garden would run dry, the same with the water butts. Then you had to get all the water from the drinking water pumps. The drinking water was hard water; the water from the water butts and garden wells was soft water, which was a lot better to wash and also to wash all the clothes in.

Electricity Supply

Electricity came into the village in 1935. It was the farms and tied cottages that got it first. Probably the Landlord paid for it. The ordinary rented cottages had to pay for it themselves, which some could not afford. When I lived at home we had a paraffin lamp in the middle of the table which lit the room, and it also had heat coming from it. When we went to bed we had a candle in a candlestick and had to carry it upstairs. Sometimes it would blow out and you would be left in the dark. They were the good days. As the years went by everyone had electricity as there was more money earn during the war.

<u>Shooting and Beating</u>

When I went to school, on a Saturday during the Shooting Season I would go beating. We would go just as it was getting daylight to stop the birds from escaping on to someone else's land. I would go along to the Rome or The Grove which was on the road from Sidestrand to Southrepps. The land for shooting belonged to the Rev Arthur Buxton. They would start shooting about 9.30am. We would join in with them when they joined up with us. We would have our dinner near Keepers Cottage which is no longer there, which is the Woodland Caravan Site and owned by the Harrison family. Us boys got 3 shillings and the men got 6 shillings a day.

Wartime Shortages

Food during the Second War, living in the country we were lucky as we grew our own vegetables. We also kept chickens for eggs and also ate the poultry. Food for the chickens was not easy to get. If you worked on a farm you got extra rations for haymaking and harvest. You had to have your tea in the fields. The extra rations were for sugar, tea and flour, every little helped. During the War we lived on spam, you could also get dried egg, which we had never heard of before the War. It was not an easy life; every house was in darkness from the outside. If a little light was seen you would be had up as the Police were always on the look out, which was quite right.

Horses

When I started work on the farm in 1940 it was all horse work. We used to get the horses ready with harnesses on, when it came to put on the collar some horses would lift their heads up so high I could not reach. I had to stand in the manger. When we were ready we would go off in the fields for the day with a bag of hay for the horses for their dinner. I would sit on the bank and have my dinner. The work could be harrowing, rolling, drilling manure or carrying muck which was set about the fields in heaps and later spread by fork and ploughed in. If it was wet I would have a sack on my shoulders and one around my waist to keep dry, no waterproofs in those days.

Letter from Alec

I would like to thank the people who live at No 16 Church Street. It was an awful night and I sat indoors by the fire and watched a great firework display through my window. It lasted half an hour or more and it was fantastic. Thank you. To think when I was small it was little demons, jumping jacks and Catherine wheels, all very small compared with today, they would last about 5 minutes.

2017

Alec's Mum Florrie

Pilgrim Shelter 1935 with Rev Page

The Village Halls in Trimingham

The first was the laundry at The Old Rectory on Station Corner, which ran alongside the road. The School at Buxton Hall was a popular building for the Village. It was used for Whist Drives, Dances, Parties, Council Meetings and Sea Scouts etc. Then, of course, the Pilgrim Shelter which was built as a Men's Club and which is now being used for everything. It is not big enough. I hope that the new one will be supported well after all the hard work the people have put into it. I look forward to seeing it built and used.

Wash Day

Wash day in our house when I was young: Mother would fill the copper with water from a pump in the back yard. The copper was in the wash house, which was also in the back yard. She would then put sticks and coal in the furnace and light it. It would then boil the water. She would be working indoors until it had boiled. During the day she would put some of the linen in the copper to boil while she washed the other items by hand and then wrung them out by hand. In later years she got a wringer which you cranked around by hand, then hung them out to dry and then ironed them. This was not very nice during the winter. To keep the copper boiling they would use bits of wood, old shoes etc. When ironing they had to heat the iron on the fire to get hot, no electricity or mains water then.

More Tractors

The first tractor I drove was a Standard Ford, and several of their makes as the years went on. The one I drove the longest was a Grey Ferguson. The first one was all petrol, then petrol and kerosene oil. Then it was diesel. I done the deep ploughing for sugar beet and all the other tractor work. I ploughed Cromer Golf Course up, the bit which was behind Overstrand Convalescent Home and ran towards Overstrand along the cliff. When I think of the size of the tractors of today compared with the little Grey Ferguson! The back wheels of the modern tractors were as big as the little Grey. The Grey was a marvellous machine with all its own implements made by Ferguson such as ploughs, springtine harrows, corn drills, cultivators etc.

Elephants

When I was a lad in the village, it was not too long ago (wishful thinking), there were Circuses in North Walsham, Mundesley and Cromer. North Walsham is where the Swimming Pool now is, Mundesley as you walked from the village to the Station, where Munhaven is and Cromer was also at Cromwell Road on the left-hand side from Overstrand Road to Norwich Road. They used to walk the Elephants to the different fields. I can remember them walking through Trimingham, what a size! Not much traffic then of course. On long distances they would put the elephants in Lorries to move them. On the same fields they would hold Fairs.

Pits and Chicks

The Gravel Pit in Middle Street was opened after the War. When I worked at Beacon Farm where the Gravel Pit is now there was a small hole in the land and it was full of gorse bushes. The Farmer at Beacon Farm had wire netting around it and kept poultry in it. They were big poultry farmers. In the field in front of the farm they had big poultry houses. The first one was for day old chicks and it held hundreds. As they got older, they would move to the other big sheds. There were more sheds where the bungalows in Middle Street are going back to the gravel pit. There was a lot of sand carted out of the pit for Bacton Gas Site when it was being built.

Beet Season

One morning I looked out of the window, it was foggy and frosty and I sat next to a lovely fire. I thought back to when I first started work during the Sugar Beet Season, we would go in the field at 7.00am digging the beet by hand. You had a short-handle fork with two tines, you pushed it in the ground with one hand and grabbed the top with the other. You would be there in all weathers, no waterproof gloves and your hands and feet would be frozen. You would sit on the bank to eat your dinner and be in the field until it was dark. The season lasted from end of September until the end of December. How times have changed.

Light Fingers

How times change. I have lived in the village all my life and never locked shed doors only the house door at night. But over the last few years I have lost an extension ladder, extension electric lead. A while ago I went shopping and locked the inside door but left the porch door unlocked and when I returned the porch door was open and I lost something out of the porch. The porch door is now also always locked. So be careful out there.

Horse Dressing

A friend came to see me and he said, "I have started collecting horse harness", which was great as I worked with horses. I said to him, "Have you got a halter?" – which fitted over the face and head, then the collar which had sails on. The collar went over the horse's head upside down, then twisted around to its shoulders, the sails were of wood, had a top bond and a bottom tightened up to keep it in place. There was a short chain fitted to the sails called *tees,* they were used for tumbrels, which was a cart. The next thing was a saddle fitted on the horse's back. It was made of strong material stuffed with straw with wood on top. It had a channel in for a chain to fit in. Then came the breeches fitted on the back of the horse. The halter and the reins were to start the horse, the collar was for pulling, the saddle to take the weight. The beeches were made for backing; they were joined together with leather straps.

Wells

The Drinking Water wells listed below were from Springs. Most houses had a pump for the soft water from the roof of the property which was used for personal washing and clothes washing. These wells were the only water supply for the village:

The Cottage (Coastguard Officer's House); Coastguard Cottages; Council Houses; Station Yard (which was used by the Station House and Cottages); The Old Rectory; Blackberry Hall; Keeper's Cottage; Hall Farm (also supplied Cow House and Diary); From top of back garden of No 8 The Street (supplied the houses on The Street); The Shop; Pilgrim House; Grange Farm (now known as Church Farm); Bottledene; Farm on the Old Road; Greystones; Beacon Farm (two wells); Crown & Anchor; Cliffside; Opposite Jenny Cooper's (used to supply Middle Street); Highlawns; Four Winds; Bonnyrigg.

More Rabbiting

When I was a young lad in the winter on a Saturday afternoon and Sunday morning I would go rabbiting with my Dad and his brother. We would have all the equipment such as ferrets, long-handled spades and nets. Sometimes the ferrets would be on a long line and sometimes they would be coped which meant they would have a bit of string around their mouth and then tied around the back of their head so that they could not bite the rabbit. This was when the nets were used, the rabbits were chased by the ferret and they would get caught in the nets. The rabbit made a good meal. Mother used to skin them and bake them. A man came around the villages and bought the skins for one penny and sometimes two pennies.

Changes and Closures

For the people who have not lived long in the village; many years ago we had 2 shops, also a butcher's shop, pub and school. The school closed in 1930 to 1931. We also had a Chapel and it was well attended. When the Chapel was first closed it was used as a First Aid Depot by St Johns Ambulance. My brother, Len, was keen on first aid and he spent his working life in that line. All the farms had horses, cows and pigs which were lovely to see and hear. Of course we had a railway and coal yard and coal was delivered to the villages. Sugar Beet went by rail and cattle to Norwich market

Squatters

When the Loop Road was so you could walk round it, it was on a Sunday evening and it was getting dark, I was taking the dog for a walk. When I got to Greystones the big room was lit up. I thought how strange as Greystones had not been lived in for a long while, so I took a glance in the window. There was this boy sitting by the fire. I went to see my brother-in-law who lived next door. I said, "Would you phone the Police and come with me?" and I told him why. We spoke to the boy and he said he was on the Duke of Edinburgh award scheme. I said to him, "Do you go into empty property?" and he said, "Yes." We kept him talking until the Police arrived. They took him to North Walsham Police Station. He had escaped from Borstal in Portsmouth.

2018

Alec with his Gang

Alec's Gang in Demolition Mode

Plough Shares

It was where Mrs Reid lives at Grange Cottage (as it is now known) the Farmers used to have the horses shod and it was big business then. The Farmers also had the plough shares and cultivator blades and harrow tines repaired. The house was then turned into a house. The house went with the farm near the Church as a tied cottage. The Farmer who had the farm was a Mr Robert Page and his son Claude lived in the cottage with his wife Maud and they had 2 children, David and Iris. Of course Claude worked on the farm for his Father and also Claude's brother Norman. They worked there until the Estate was sold up and Claude bought the house he lived in and that is where he finished his days.

Carborundum

Dot came to see and she was carrying something in her hand. She said, "What is this? I found it in a drawer in the Church." It was a carborundum. It could have been my Dad's. When he used a scythe he would have used it to sharpen the blade. When he mowed the Churchyard he used a scythe. It could be used to sharpen the hives of a hay cutter, a binder, and hives for cutting corn. The type of hives used now do not need sharpening. Sometimes you would have used it to sharpen a hook for hedging. The one Dot showed me had a wooden handle which was expensive. The one Dad used mostly for a hook did not have a handle.

Youth Employment

I left school at 13, as my 14th birthday came in the holidays. I started work at Hall Farm, it was Harvest time. This is a nice time on a farm. I went to Beacon Farm as I was loaned out. I worked among the poultry; there were hundreds from day-olds to laying hens. My Uncle was Foreman. I stayed there for 2 years, and then I went back to Hall Farm. After a time Church Farm could not get a cowman so I went there to help out, then I went back to Hall Farm. After that I went to Bizewell Farm for 2 years, and then I went and worked for the War Agricultural Department. I was picked up by lorry and we went around different farms, there were about 20 of us. Some did not know much about farm work, I was put in charge of a gang of 5. We got on very well as they had worked on farms.

We did sugar beeting, potato picking, and draining, building bridges over the dykes. I was there for 6 months. I left and got a job on a farm at Ivy Farm, Sidestrand and was there for 17 years. I done milking, looking after the cattle, all tractor work, stacking straw and corn stacks and thatching. The combine then came in which I drove and stacking ceased. I drove various makes of tractors, the one I drove the longest were Fergusson.

When I left Ivy Farm I went and worked for Norfolk County Council and stayed for 28 years. I started at the Holt Depot, then North Walsham, Stalham and finished at Caister. I worked in most of the villages and shopping centre in Norfolk. I had a lorry and I picked men up and we did roadwork. I was in charge of a gang which could be from 2 men to 10.

School Days

Buxton Hall was the school; it was left to the village by Rev Buxton who owned most of the village. The school was left to be used as a Village Hall and it was used for a number of years. It was used for Whist Drives, Dances, Concerts, Parties – Christmas, Weddings and Birthdays. Trimingham Sea Scouts also used it and I was one. At the front which joins the road was a big flag pole, it had been a ship's mast and had 4 guy ropes to support it. It took up all the front area. We used to fly the flags and the international code flags. The school was sold as Trimingham could not afford to run 2 halls, so they kept Pilgrim Shelter. The school was turned into living accommodation which got the name Buxton Hall.

Autobiography Part 1

I left school and started work at Hall Farm for Mr C Harrison. It was harvest time; most of the work was done by horse then. When you started in a field of corn you had to mow about six foot wide around the headline so when the binder came in it was clean. Before that the men that had mowed had to tie the corn in shoves and laid it on the hedge.

After the binder had done six rounds around the field you would set the shoves up and continue until the field was done. After that the drag-rake would rake up all the loose, it would be put in rows, nothing was wasted. Then it was all put in stacks. Later on the corn would get thrashed and then it got sold to the corn merchants. The straw was used for the cattle. After the fields got cleared you would cut the hedges with a hook, all the cuttings would be cleared and used for stack bottoms or covering the mangold hales to keep the frost out. I was lent out to Beacon Farm.

They kept hundreds of poultry and my job was looking after them. We had day-old chicks which were kept under cover with an oil lamp to keep them warm. Then we had the different ages up to the laying hens. In the winter time the laying hens used to have warm water to drink first thing. They had meal to eat which had cod liver oil mixed in. After all the poultry had been fed they had to be cleaned out. Fresh sawdust for the little chicks and straw for the laying hens. I had to collect the eggs three times a day. It was a busy life. The poultry houses were on the field on the opposite side of the road to the farmhouse and in Middle Street where the bungalows and sandpit are now. I worked there for two years.

Autobiography Part 2

Then I worked at Bizewell Farm for two years as a general farm worker. The farmer was Mr Hicks. He was always well behind getting anything done, all the other farmers would have finished harvest before he had started, but he got through life. Then I worked for the War Agricultural and I used to catch a lorry at Overstrand. When we had picked up all the men we would go to Matlaske to the German Prison of War Camp. We would pick up the tools we needed to use. We would go to different farms to do draining, sugar beating and looking after the potatoes etc. We also worked on Coltishall Aerodrome. I worked there for six months.

Next I got to work at Ivy Farm, Sidestrand. It was horse and tractor work and after a while it was all tractor. The machinery was converted for tractor use. We grew barley, oats, wheat, sugar beet, cauliflowers, cucumbers, peas, daffodils and tulips. The fields of corn were all cut with a binder, put in stacks and threshed. In later years it was all combined. I used all the machinery on the farm such as ploughing, drillings, combining etc. Daffodils were grown for the bulbs, also the tulips. The flower heads had to be picked at certain time before they died off. The cucumbers went to the pickling factory, also the cauliflowers. The peas were picked and sold at local shops. The sugar beet went to Cantley, some by train and some by road. There was also a big herd of Friesian cows, the milk went by road to the Milk Marketing Board at Norwich. I did the milking when the cowman had his day off or holiday. If the farm was busy the Farmer would do the milking so I could keep working on the land. Then I thought I would have a change of work.

Autobiography Part 3

I went to Norfolk County Council Highways. I started off working with different gangs doing new roads and widening some. In between I was roadman for the villages near home. Then I got a lorry. We had a hut on the back which the men travelled in. There were five in the gang which I was in charge of with the work that needed doing. We went around the villages every thirteen weeks doing pot holes, edging the road sides, footpaths, draining. Sometimes we would get an emergency call, that was most weekends or night time. Winter time it would be gritting and snow ploughing.

When I first started we would have to go to Holt to get the salt, it was anytime from midnight onwards. My depot was at Holt where we would get the tarmac etc, also tools. I ended up at Stalham Depot. Going back to when I worked on the farm; we grew daffodils and after they were taken up they went into a riddle which separated the bulbs so all the big bulbs went into trays and the small one thrown into a heap to rot away. The trays of bulbs were loaded onto a big trailer and taken to a farm to be sterilised to get rid of any disease. They were put into boiling water in wire baskets into big tanks which had had a chemical put into it. They would be in for a certain time, after all that we would go and collect them and they were then ready for planting.

Trosh

I was reading in the Newsletter that Trimingham is having a Trosh Day. I have done several weeks of that in the past which we called Threshing. The Threshing Machine was a steam engine, a drum, straw-pitcher and a chaff-cutter. It was a great sight to see the machines going through the village to the farms. The men would hang their bicycles on the back of the straw-pitcher. When the machine was sat next to the corn stack they could then cycle to and from the site, some had to cycle long distances and there was a man who lived in Middle Street who walked following the machine from farm to farm. They used to have to have the steam up ready for 7.30am when the men started work. The farmer, if he threshed on a Monday, the start of the week, had to pay the insurance for the week. They were not too happy to thresh on a Monday. It was alright if you got a whole week's threshing to do. It was only the big farmers who did that.

The Farmers had to employ extra staff to do the job. There would be the engine driver to make sure he kept a good fire going. There would be 2 men on the drum, one cutting the bonds with a special knife from the corn sheaves; the other man would be feeding the sheaves into the drum. The drum threshed the corn out. There would be one man sacking the corn and weighing it. If it was oats it would be 12 stone, barley 16 stone and wheat 18 stone. There would be one sacking the chaff which came from the corn heads, there would be 2 or 3 men on the corn stack pitching to the bond-cutter. Also

2 men on the straw stack which was bedding for cattle.

During threshing there would be 2 men with horse and cart taking the sacks of the corn to the barn and one man with a horse and cart carrying the chaff for winter feed for the cattle. During the day horse-drawn water carts came to supply water for the engine. This was all done before tractors took over the carting work and the steam engine. During the war they had to put wire netting around the corn stacks to stop the rats from escaping which the men killed with a pitch fork or the farm dogs did. I should have mentioned before starting threshing, the thatch to keep it dry had to be taken off.

2019

Alec & Margaret, Spot-the-Ball Winners 1

Alec & Margaret, Spot-the-Ball Winners 2

Puruzi Ice Cream

I was reading the EDP and saw the death of a man whose Mum and Dad used to come to the village on Saturdays and Sundays selling ice cream. The name was Mr & Mrs Puruzi. I mentioned to them that this village was having a Fete. I went to Norwich to get some ice cream from them and they put it in a container which kept it from melting. The vehicle I went in was a Red Cross Ambulance belonging to Dr Barnardos. When I got back to the village it poured with rain all afternoon and so the fete was cancelled. So that the ice cream was not wasted we went around the village and gave it away. Not a lot of profit made on that day.

Dogs

Dogs were a big part of my life. After I got married when we came back home after our honeymoon we had a dog and two cats waiting for us. The cats' names were Minnie and Mushon, they were pure white and he was called Rover. We then had a long while when we only had cats, as my wife loved animals. The next dog was a Cairn

Terrier and Honey was her name, she came from Dereham in a tea chest and we picked her up from Trimingham Station. We had her for 13 years when she died. Then we had another Cairn Terrier and we went near Holt to get her and had her for 17 years. Next was a black Labrador and we went near Attleborough to get her, she was 12 when she died.

While we had her I was near Coltishall and a lady came along with three children and a Golden Labrador. One of the men in my gang just laughed and said to her, "Do you want to sell the dog?" and she said, "Yes", as her husband was in the Air Force and was being posted to Germany but it would not be for a few weeks. We exchanged names and phone numbers and about 3 days later to my surprise she phoned to say I could have the dog. We went and got her and she got on the back seat with Peggy, a bit of swearing went on but they soon got to love each other. Her name was also Honey and she lived until she was 13.

The next one was a Golden Labrador. We went to the Dogs Home in Drayton Road Norwich. It was six months old and had been put in the home because the owners had split up. The Manager of the Dogs Home phoned us and told us about her because my wife raised a lot of money for that Home. He was a loving dog and we had him for 8 years, he died of cancer. The next was a Black Labrador and her name was Cassie. We went to Mildenhall to get her. I said to my wife "No" but she said "Yes". We were taking her to give her a good life as the place was a breeding kennels; they were just interested in the money. We brought her home and she was 18 when she died. But now I am left with no animals, only china ones. What a big miss in life!

<u>Cromer</u>

It was a good thing going into Cromer by train, bus, bicycle and much later by car. If you went on your bike you could take it to a shop on the Overstrand Road near the traffic lights. It was a Mr Drury and you paid a penny (old money) and you knew it was safe. Another place was almost opposite to where Iceland is. It was a Mr & Mrs Beck, and the shops were on the roadside. Behind the cycle shop was the Kersel with bumper cars and slot machines etc. Along the road was a shoe repair shop which got knocked down to make the road wider. The road that goes down to the sea front beside the Church there was Rusts, down Garden Street was Mutimers. There was a Mr Huggins who came around the village to take the grocery order and a Mr Burton brought the goods a day or so after. This was for Mutimers. There were some good shops then more than now. There was the Tudor Cafe, another one near the traffic lights was Scotts, Bradley's men's outfitters, Jack Hall, the barber and Pearsons ladies hairdressers.

Railways 2

My father, Frank Reynolds, could remember sitting on the embankment at Trimingham as a little lad watching the men working. My Grandfather had told Frank that the spoils from the cutting was used for the embankments and that it would be loaded up into wagons and a small steam loco would give a sharp tap to send them down the line. Two men were assigned to fix a sprag to the wheels so that the wagon tipped its load. Sometimes they were a bit too over-enthusiastic and the entire wagon would tip right over. Since it could not easily be righted it would be buried in the embankment. Frank said, "I suppose more than one is still there."

Cliff Falls and Water

I have just read about another cliff fall. I know we have had a lot of rain but what about all the springs in the ground which used to supply the drinking water from the pumps or wells for all the houses etc, before the water main was installed. The water is still in the ground somewhere. If all the springs were tapped, think of the amount of water that could be saved. Years ago there was a Water Diviner who came to the village. He found seven springs in the field behind the cottages in Church Street. The man's name was Mr Bloom from Southrepps. Then there is all the water which is put onto the land, which is a great volume of water, to help the crops grow. The years I worked on the farm there was no irrigation. The crops fed on the muck that was put on the land and ploughed in and fed the land. How times have changed.

The Doctors

When I was young Mum, my sister and I had a North Walsham Doctor, Dr Hart. Dr McLeod and his wife were also doctors. Dad had a Dr Morrison and the surgery was at what is now the Beechwood

Hotel in North Walsham. Early in the 1930s Dr Miller opened a surgery at St Braddock in Mundesley, so Mum, my sister and I went to Mundesley. My sister and I are still there. Dad kept at North Walsham until he died. You did not have to make an appointment, you just walked in. The first thing you did was count how many people were in the surgery so you knew when it was your turn. Sometimes the Receptionist would open the surgery door and say, "I am sorry but the Doctor has been called out for an emergency case and I do not know what time he will be back, so you can wait or come back." At that time of day the Doctor did two surgeries, one in the morning and one in the evening. He also did home visits and helped at Cromer Hospital. What a busy life he had. I find Mundesley Surgery and the staff very good.

The Cliffs

I recently read about a cliff fall at Sidestrand and saw the pictures of it and also the Trimingham sea defences. What a disgrace to let them get in such a state. To think how the sea defences have protected Trimingham cliffs all these years and now they are left to breakaway and also the money it cost to install them. I can always remember my Dad saying that they had been working on the cliff top pulling swedes for cattle food, it was a horse and cart at that time. They left off for dinner, and fed and watered the horses. When they had finished their dinner they returned to the field on the cliff top and where they had been working that morning it had all fallen down onto the beach. It was about an acre of land.

Sugar Beet

To think when I worked on the farm in the sugar beet fields you would see men hoeing the beet so they would be about 8 inches apart, everyone single. We would start hoeing the second week in May and finish the first week in July. After they had been hoed once you would start again hoeing the acres you had done, looking for any weeds or if you had left a double plant. When the seed was drilled you got four or five plants from one seed which was like a cluster. All the hard work and back ache have now gone, a sprayer does the work now.

Straw Stack Fires

One day when I was cycling home from work and I got near the caravan site entrance, I happened to look across to the sea. So far across, near White Gate Lane, there was a big straw stack with children playing on top of it. The next time I looked across there were flames coming from the top of the straw stack. The next thing I saw was the children running towards the cliff to hide in the Plantation Wood. They were not found when they were being looked for. Also they were very lucky they never burned as a straw stack burns very quickly.

In the same place during the war, there was a straw stack and most of it was used for the cattle. The rest was set alight to burn it and the rubbish that was left around it. When it got a good fire going there was ammunition flying about as the area was the battle area. The soldiers put the live ammunition in the stack so that they did not have to fire it and got back home quicker.

Players Please

The other day my cousin Tom had come to see me, he lives in Maidstone in Kent but he was born in Trimingham. We got talking about old cars. He said that he went to a Vintage Car Show and he was talking about the different makes. He mentioned one that was called "All Days and Onions", which brought back memories because a farmer that farmed at Bizewell Farm had one of that make. His name was Mr Hicks. Nearly every time he went out in it he ran out of petrol. The most he used it for was to come up to the Trimingham shop to get his cigarettes, which were Players. In later years I worked for him for about two years. He was a farmer well behind other farmers, drilling at harvest time, he would start when all the others had finished.

2020

Edwin in Uniform

Edwin's Service Certificate

Alec with his Dad Frank

Treasure Trove

My brother-in-law, Alan, was a great in-law. He would always help me if he could. He was a good man; it is over a year ago since he died. He was a builder. He built his own bungalow, and he would have a Tilley lamp to work by. He worked all day for a builder. Later he worked for himself and built the bungalows each side of his and several others in nearby villages. He was an excellent tradesman. When he was a little boy he heard people talking about putting money in the bank. He had saved a tin full of farthings so he thought he would put them in the bank. He went up his garden, dug a hole in the bank and put the tin with the farthings in it. He told his Dad what he had done and he went to find it but never did. I expect the tin fell into a rabbit's burrow, they are still there somewhere.

Shooting

When I was younger and fitter I used to go on Mr Harrison's estate. When I first started I went as a beater with a flag which you waved to make the birds fly high. I would line up in front of the guns, the other beaters would drive the woods shouting and rattling sticks on the trees. When you had done that plantation, you would move to the next. In later years Mr Harrison said, "Why don't you drive the tractor with a trailer on and transport the beaters and the man in charge of them?" I did this until I was unable to do it any more. The man in charge would tell me where to drop the beaters. They would spread out in a line and wait until the guns got into position, the whistle would be blown and the shoot would start. The shoot would start about 9.00am and finish about 4.00pm. When I was at school if there was a shoot on a Saturday I would go and we would start just before it got light. We would try to stop the birds flying onto neighbouring land. The pay was 3 shillings for a boy and 10 shilling for a man.

Overstrand School

When I went to school at Overstrand, when you got to 11 years old the girls went to cookery classes. There was a big cookery room which was part of the school. The boys went to carpentry classes at Cromer School. We had to walk there and back. Sometimes a lady from Overstrand, called Miss Vannop, would pick us up and took us back to school. The car was a big sports car, which we thought was great. My sister went to cookery classes, which was on a Friday and she would cook our dinner. This was a change from sandwiches. It was not nice for the other boys who did not have a sister; they did not get a cooked lunch. The cookery teacher came from Dereham, she had an Austin 7 saloon. One Friday she took 3 of us boys to North Lodge Park where the Crown Jewels were on show. She paid for us to go in. In Dereham there was a big tractor firm called J J Wright and I think she had something to do with it.

Gas Power

I read recently that the Government is going to try and stop vehicles using petrol and diesel. This made me remember that during the Second World War our local buses had to pull a small two-wheeled trailer behind it which had containers of gas in it. The gas was used to run the bus. There was a Harley Street specialist doctor, Dr Open, who lived in Middle Street and he had to travel to London for his clinic and had his car converted to gas and the gas tank was in the boot. His wife used to collect the money for War Bonds, a few pennies each week and when you had paid £1 you got a Certificate and after 5 years it was worth one pound and 5 shillings.

My family

I had one sister and two brothers. Edwin was the youngest, then Len, then me and then Daphne. Edwin was a carpenter; Len was a male nurse in a hospital. Daphne worked in munitions during the war. I worked half my life on farms and the rest for Norfolk Highways. When Len was two years old he got diphtheria, so Daphne and I had to go to live with an Uncle and Aunt in Trimingham, two doors up from home. Then after a fortnight Len went into the Isolation Hospital at Roughton. He stayed there for a month; he was lucky to get over it. Dad biked over every night and peeped through a window to see him. It was brought to the village by some boys on holiday. I had an Uncle who got it too. So after that my sister and I went back home. Edwin died, Len lives in Leicester, Daphne is in a home at Brundall. I have stayed in the village where I was born with the help of Dot and Sue

Deliveries and Trade

As I sit in my conservatory it reminds me of years ago as you see the delivery vans stopping at the houses or going past to other villages. Years ago there would be vans delivering groceries, bread, cakes, fish, and milk. Also there were lorries delivering coal, poultry, food etc.

These vehicles came from Mundesley, North Walsham, Southrepps, Cromer, and Overstrand. There was also a pony with a flat cart with fruit and vegetables from Trunch and a pony and trap with milk. Cromer it was Mutimers with groceries, a Mr Huggins came and got the order and a Mr Burton delivered them a week later. Also International

Stores and Rusts dealt in groceries and clothes. From Overstrand Hardy the Baker, Southrepps Drury a Baker, Mundesley Gedge the Baker, before him it was Mr Burton and his bake house went down the cliff. Milk was delivered by Twigg, and then the Milk Marketing Board took over.

Other milkmen were Williams of Gimingham and Mr White from Fen Farm Southrepps, he had a pony and trap and had his own cows. When he sold his herd of cows he got his milk to sell from Mr Harrison, Hall Farm. Mr White gave all the children in the village an orange at Christmas, which we got at the Christmas Party in the school, which was Buxton Hall. There was a fish monger in the village which delivered around the villages. First he had a motor bike and sidecar and later a van. They also came from Yarmouth on a Saturday morning with fish.

Rags and Bones

I hope everyone is coping well with this virus. I wish you all the best of luck and keep clear of it. I am not doing too bad. I have got good help from Dot and Sue who are marvellous to me. If it was not for them I would not be in my own house. I cannot thank them enough. I would also like to thank all the folk passing by who wave to me and also those who walk up the garden and speak to me through the window. Thank you: it means a lot to me. Years ago on a Saturday morning there was a Rag and Bone man came round the village in his horse and cart. He would shout, "Any old rags today, Mam?" He would give you a few coppers for them. He would buy rabbit skins for a penny or two pence (old money) each. It all depended on how good the fur was. A wild rabbit was a good meal before they got myxomatosis. My Dad and his brother Percy used to go rabbiting on a Saturday afternoon and Sunday morning with the ferrets. One was called Marmaduke. My Grandfather was a gamekeeper and one day my Aunt Kate when she was a little girl opened the door of the ferret hut and the ferret bit her nose. She did not get close to them after that. Some ferrets could be very vicious and if you did not hold them properly they would pin hold of you. These were working ferrets, not pets.

Scissor Grinder

I hope you are all coping well with the virus. We never thought we would have to live through a time like this. The war years were bad with the bombing and aeroplanes crashing on the way back to the airdrome after coming back from bombing the enemy. Once upon a time there was a scissor grinder who used to come to the villages on his bicycle. He had an emery wheel fitted on his handlebars. He stood the bicycle on a stand and he would sit and peddle, which drove the emery wheel and he would sharpen scissors, knives etc – the good old days. Last time I thanked people who are very very good to me; I meant to thank my neighbours Neil and Jane as they also very good to me and I wanted to thank everyone.

Harvest Time

The cornfields are turning gold which means it will soon be harvest time; just think that a combine with a trailer following and with the weather fine it is done. Years ago when I started work in the 1940s it was all done by horses. Before the binder went in the field the men would mow a swathe about 6 foot wide, then it had to be tied into sheaves, then the binder would cut the corn. You would stand the sheaves up; you would put 6 rows into one sheaf. They would stand for a while, then carted to be put into stacks. Before the War you would have four or five stacks beside each other. They had to stand separate in case of fire. The stacks had to be thatched to keep them dry. Then the next thing the thrashing machine would come to thresh (Trosh) the corn from the stacks. It would be put in sacks and put the in the barn. Think of all that work and now the whole operation is done in one go with combine and trailer and put into the barn

Cliff Tipping

I hope everyone is coping alright, good luck to everyone. As I sit in my conservatory and see the different dustcarts go past it makes me think of the time when there were none at all. I am sure there was not the amount of waste as there is now. When I was young, which is a few years ago now, I had a wheelbarrow which was a box on old pram wheels and wooden handles. We would put the rubbish into the wheelbarrow which consisted of a few tins and ash from the fire and put it over the cliff which eventually got covered up. Also garden rubbish went over the cliff and that would help to cover the tins up. I think it is a good thing for garden rubbish to go over the cliff as a lot of the rubbish would strike root and help the cliffs and you also got the flowers where the rubbish would grow so there was a bit of colour.

The first dustcart I can remember was a farmer from Mundesley, it went round the villages. It was Bertie Bullimore and his son Donny who was on it, they lived at Gimingham. There was a dump between Mundesley and Gimingham on the back road. When Mr Harrison bought Fen Farm the road to it was just a cart track. He widened it and the dustcart tipped rubbish down there, and someone who worked on the farm would level it out. It made a good foundation for the top to go on, it was a good roadway then. Then after that the rubbish was put in the railway cutting, then top soil was put on it and that land is now being cropped.

Beet Season

The harvest is over, all safely gathered in. The next thing will be the sugar beet season. When I worked on the farm we would start lifting the sugar beet September to January. Every day wet or dry we would have a fork or digger, which were made for sugar beet use only. You would have a fork or digger in one hand and you would grab the top of the beet with your other hand, pull them out of the ground, lay 4 rows in one side and four rows the other side, with a space in between. Then you scraped any leaves off to make a clean space to top the leaves off and put the beet in heaps and the tops in rows. The sugar beet were loaded on to a horse and cart or tractor and trailer. Some beet were loaded into railway wagons and some were heaped on the roadside and taken by lorry to Cantley factory. The beet tops were used to feed the cattle. That was the old days. Now they go into the field with a beet harvester which does 6 rows at a time and loads them on to a trailer and they are heaped on the roadside. The first beet harvester I used did one row at a time, it was not self-propelled, it was towed by tractor. A tractor and trailer would follow beside and the beet would go straight into it. Now the modern beet harvesters have a big tank which the beet goes into and holds a few ton which it then unloads. The potato season will soon start, taking up is all done by machinery and stored in big sheds, which years ago it was all done by hand.

Early Days

When I left school I worked at Hall Farm for Mr C Harrison. We had to work 48 hours in the winter and 52 hours in the summer for the same money. I got paid 16 shillings a weeks and out of that I had to pay for two stamps, which was for sickness and if you got unemployed. Of course it was wartime and the clocks were put on 2 hours which meant dark mornings and light longer in the afternoons. It meant as it was dark in the morning we could not start work until 8 o'clock and leave off at 6 o'clock. After a while working at Hall Farm I was loaned out to Beacon Farm and I was there for 2 years. The farmer was Mr Firman and it was looking after poultry. My Uncle Percy was foreman there. I returned to Hall Farm and was then loaned out to Church Farm. It was a Mr Page and it was to help with milking cows and feeding cattle.

After a while a girl from the village, Edith Fuller, went to work for Mr Page so I went back to Hall Farm. Then I left there and worked for Mr Hicks at Bizewell Farm for 2 years. Then I had 6 months working for the War Agricultural and we went round Norfolk to different farms doing various work. After that I went to work at Ivy Farm for

Mr Duffield for 15 years. He was a good farmer, I did every thing on that farm from using horses, all tractor work, combining, milking cows etc. Then I thought I would have a change, so I got a job with Norfolk County Council Highways and that is where I was until I retired. It makes you wonder where all the 29 years of retirement have gone.

Sea Defences

The other day my neighbour, Neal, took his dogs down on the beach. He took photos of the breakwaters and the sea defence. What a terrible mess they are in. Think of all the thousands of pounds it cost to put them there. It is a disgrace not to keep them repaired. How come villages either side of Trimingham the defences are repaired but ours is left to break away. It is a sure thing that they protected the cliff. When they put the mines in the cliff it did more harm than good. I am sure if the Germans had wanted to land along this coast they would have shelled the cliffs, and land where they wanted to.

Beach Access

Before the war there were four footpaths down to the beach. There were more fishermen in the village that got a living from the sea. They helped to keep the paths in good order. Each year they would collect wood from the beach to make steps and rails and posts where the slopes were. How times have changed. The footpath to the beach got used a lot. People would be swimming, paddling, playing ball games and some would be sleeping, soaking up the sun and waking up rather sun burnt.

2021

Alec with Sister Daphne & Alan Self

Sheila, Dot & Sue

Christmas Memories of Alice

I hope you are all coping with this terrible virus. As I am writing this mardle you will be looking forward to Christmas, I am sure the children will. When I was small we never got a lot but we appreciated what we did get. There was not a lot of money in the village. In those days it was working on farms or building trade, some men it was seasonal work about seven months a year. You did not get very fat from the Labour Exchange, but everyone seemed quite happy. Going back to Christmas, Alice kept the shop in Church Street and served the village well, the buildings are now 3 cottages, one was the shop, one a tea rooms and the other was living accommodation. The tea room was turned into a Christmas shop with a tree and all Christmas things to buy.

After my sister and I had gone to bed Alice would bring us a Christmas present. At that time Christmas would start Christmas Eve when the trees would get decorated, Mother would be busy baking cakes and stuffing the cockerel. Of course a month before Christmas they would make Christmas pudding and Christmas cake. Christmas Day just as it got dusk we would go for a walk and see the Christmas trees with the candles flickering in the windows on the branches of the trees, there was no electricity in the village then. All the baking and cooking was done in a cooking range which was coal-burning and was in the kitchen. In the other room was an open fire which always had a big log on it which would burn for a long while and gave a good heat out and it was nice and warm.

Winter Months

I expect the sugar beet season is coming to the end. Today they go into the field with a sugar beet harvest and it is all done in one go. When I started work on the farm in 1940 sugar beet was dug out by hand. It took from the end of September and we looked to finish the end of December. Then we would start ploughing the land for the spring crops such as barley and oats. The only land ploughed in winter months would be for winter wheat. When it was threshed the straw would be used for thatching the other corn stacks to keep the water out. It was a skilled job and it was the team man that would do it. Some winters if you got a lot of snow the men that worked on farms or other outdoor work would be employed by the County Council for digging out the snowdrifts. This was done by shovel, no machinery to do the jobs in those days. I still think they were the good days when you look back. The cowman and cattle feeders stayed on the farm to make sure the cattle were fed, watered and had plenty of straw to lay on and a rack full of good hay to eat. There was nothing that looked better than to see cattle looking warm and happy.

Gritters and Snow-Ploughs

As I sit writing it is snowing and it reminds me of my working days. I spent 28 years with the Council gritting and snow ploughing. When I worked on the farm I used to grit the roads with a tractor and trailer, a local council worker spread the sand from the back of the trailer. First we would do the road from Sidestrand to Mundesley which was the main road. We would then do the byroads. We had sand piled along the road, all done by hand. When I worked for the Council it was all done by machine. I would travel to Holt in the lorry with the gritter behind filled up with salt, and then do the A and B roads. We would then do the C roads and minor roads and housing estates.

Snow Hazard

On the way to Holt I would pick up men from Thorpe Market, Roughton and Cromer as I had a crew cab there was enough room for 5, I started off at Holt, then Hanworth and Worstead. At Caister there was the depot where the salt was kept. Now the whole area is done from Aylsham. Some days we would start gritting at 5.00am until 8.00pm. Then the next morning I would leave home at 3.30am and I would not get home until the next morning and I would sleep most of the day and then start again the next day. One morning I left home, picked up my man from Thorpe Market and got stuck in a snow drift. The snow built up back of us. The lorry was stuck there for days, so I had no lorry. Mr Harrison let me have a tractor and a driver and we went around checking on the contractor who had a bulldozer and digger to make sure they were clearing the most essential roads before moving on to the other ones. Roll on spring.

Spring Time

It was nice to see the snow go, let's hope it is the lot for this winter, but March can be a month of all weathers. It is just about Spring, a lot of people say Spring starts on the first of March. I was also told it started on 21st March. The farmers will soon be planting potatoes and sugar beet and other spring crops. When I worked on the farm, which was a long while ago, it was a nice time of year to see the land cultivated and drilled and the crops growing. The farm workers from other farms would see how straight the row were across the fields, then have a good criticise if good or not so good. In my time on the farm all crops were put in in the spring, the only winter crop was wheat. How times have changed. You never went in the field with the drill until the land had been cultivated both ways and you always drilled the opposite way the land had been cultivated the last time. The fields were much smaller then, the biggest would be about 20 acres, and most were about 5 acres upward. Each field had bank hedges and trees around them. The wet land had ditches against the bank. The hedges were cut by hand with a reef hook and ditches were dug out by hand.

Mechanisation

What a big change in farm work, also the size of machinery. To think when I started it was all horse work. You went into the field at 7.30am and came out at 5.00pm. You would be walking all day, sit on the bank and have your dinner. The horse would have a bag of hay. No heated tractor to sit in with a comfortable seat.

Spring Preparations

The time of year has come when the flowers are coming out making a bit colour which brightens the garden up, daffodils, grape hyacinths, tulips and primroses. The trouble is the weeds grow quicker. The other day Sue took me for my second jab at North Walsham, it was very busy. It was a lot busier than the first time I went. It was well organised inside and the staff pleasant. On the way there and back it was nice to see the countryside and to see the fields turning green. It was the first time I had been out of the house since December, worst of getting old. I was surprised to see a big heap of sugar beet on the roadside. I thought the factories would be closed by now, I expect it was too wet to get the beet out of the ground.

This time of year, when I went to school, everybody would start setting the vegetables, either Good Friday or Easter Monday, as you only got one day's holiday. It was like that when I started work. Going back to setting vegetables, all the ground was dug to produce food, not a lawn or grass cutter to be seen. Most of the men worked on farms, the pay was not great, so growing their own vegetables helped the funds and everything was fresh, straight out of the ground and into the pot.

Garage Costs and Motoring Memories

It is a sure thing there is a lot more traffic about. My car insurance is now due which is done by computer. When I first started motoring the garage you dealt with did the insurance for you. I suppose different garages would be Agents for different companies. It was good the price of my insurance, the price I pay now you could have bought a brand new car then, that is the worst of getting old. When I started motoring, the road tax was £12.50 and insurance was less than £1.50. The wages were not great, there were not many rich workmen but you did not need an escort home on pay day. When you look back people were happy, you knew everyone in the village you lived in and the surrounding villages. You would meet up with people from other villages and enjoy playing football, darts, dances, whist drives etc. It was all entertainment.

Feeding the Birds

I have got a lot of good birds in the garden. In one of the bird boxes are blue tits. There is one blue tit as soon as the car is parked on the path it sits and pecks at the glass in the wing mirror. When the car is gone it pecks at the window of the house. This morning as I lay in my bed, it was about quarter to five, it was pecking at the window beside my bed.

The Turning Year

How quick the year is passing, soon it will be the longest day. The weather has not been great, but it seems to be improving now. Whatever the weather the weeds grow quicker than anything, I asked my gardener if he planted them so he could keep working. When I was able to do the garden myself the flower borders would be full of bloom. The vegetable garden would see us through most of the year with meals; you cannot beat vegetables straight out of soil. In November I would set out shallots, broad beans, winter lettuce and sweet peas. They would get a good hold of root and by the spring you would have a lovely row of sweet peas full in bloom and the onions, beans and lettuce early. In February I would set other vegetables, potatoes and green vegetables. Runner beans were the last thing to set and when I set them I would sprinkle some sweet peas seed and they would flower when the other row had finished.

Visitors and Chat

The other day a friend of mine, Sheila, came from Stalham and done some cleaning. When she finished we had a game of crib and sat talking about old days, mind she cannot go back by a long way as me. We got talking about Scouts. She was a cub leader after the war and I was a sea scout before the war. We got talking about semaphore; you had two flags and sent out messages. Sheila done the same, she did not do Morse code. I am very lucky to have Sheila, Dot and Sue, they have been marvellous to me, and still are. I would not be living in Trimingham now if it was not for them. This week I had a visit from my cousin Tom and his wife Pearl, they come from Kent. Tom was born in

Trimingham near The Green, at the mouth of Middle Street. They moved to Keeper's Cottage, which is no longer there, Tom's father was the gamekeeper.

When Rev Buxton died the Trimingham Estate, that he owned, was sold and Tom's parents and him moved to Gunton Hall. I lost touch with him, but when I cut the turf for the new hall it was in the newspaper and farmer said to Tom, "Do you know him?" The next day Tom and Pearl came to see me and we have been in touch ever since. He was caravanning in Norfolk at the time the photo was shown to him. The biggest part of my life now I spend in the conservatory, a lot of people walk by and wave to me or walk up the path and talk to me, which means a lot to me. I also sleep a lot, but I tell people I am resting my eyes. Properties in the village seem to sell quite quickly. Years ago you knew everyone, but I don't know many people now as I don't get out.

Doctors 2

I have heard of people complaining about not being able to get a doctor. A friend of mine was not well, also her husband. They phoned Mundesley Surgery and got an appointment within the hour. They both went and saw the doctor, and got good attention and were very satisfied. A day or two later her husband was full of pain, they phoned the surgery and got an appointment straight away. He went to see the doctor who was very good and He got a scan at Norfolk & Norwich Hospital in a short time. That is a credit to Mundesley Surgery. I have been registered with them for eighty years or more and they keep a check on me.

Seed Time and Harvest

The year is creeping away; the weather has been poor for August so far which is bad for the harvest as the corn needs light, wind and sunshine to ripen. There is an old saying "There is always a seed time and a harvest time". There seem to be a lot of peas growing in the area now, which was a big thing years ago, but much slower getting the crop in as it was cut by machine then loaded on the trailers. Now it is all done with the pea viners and taken to the factory.

Silence and Moles

I have just had my 95th birthday, in August, and would like to thank everyone for my birthday cards, which mean a lot when you cannot get out. Also the people who came to see me, 95 years is a long time to live in the same village. I expect the harvest is all done now. It is done earlier now as most of the corn is drilled in the winter. Years ago it was only wheat drilled in the winter, barley and oats in the spring, the varieties are altogether different now. Mr Hicks, who farmed Bizewell Farm, was harvesting on Armistice Day, 11th November. He said to the men at 11.00am, "Let us have two minutes silence."

We eventually finished the harvest. Sometimes it was done by horse and sometimes by man power. Neil, my neighbour, keeps my grass cut, which looks nice and tidy. The last few days I have had a mole making molehills. I have been told that some live 6 years underground, but mostly 2 years; not much of a life underground all the time. Years ago my Dad used to catch them, skin them and send the skins to London, I don't know where but they were made into Ladies Moleskin coats. It must have taken a lot of skins to make a coat. The sugar beet season will soon start again; also the potato crop will be lifted.

The Days Shorten

Hello everyone, are you getting on alright and keeping clear of the virus? I understand that some food supplies are a bit scarce. I hope you are all managing to get what you need. What a terrible world to live in. It is worse that the wars years, we were rationed so we all got the same. The people who lived in the countryside were lucky because we had a garden and grew a lot of vegetables which went a long way. The year is going by fast, it is halfway through October and already the days are short with the dark mornings and then you get the long dark evenings. Sue and Dot are very good to me, also Neal, my neighbour, and Sheila and Allan from Stalham. I expect the potato harvest is well underway, being carted and stored. The sugar beet will have started; some will have been taken to the Beet Factory already. The corn harvest is all gathered in and some of the corn fields for next year are already drilled and up, a lovely green.

Today I was asleep in my conservatory, there was a tap on the door, and when I had finished resting my eyes, it was a man I worked with fifty years ago on the Council. He lives in Dereham, him and his wife had been for a meal at the Vernon Arms, Southrepps, which was very good. They came in and we had a good chat, talking about workmates who are getting a bit thin as a lot have passed away. It was nice to see them.

My Sister Daphne

On 17th October my sister, Daphne, died. She lived in the village the biggest part of her life, about 91 years. She was born at Northrepps, as her mother went there to a friend's house, that's where she was born. When she was about a fortnight old she came to The Buildings in Trimingham, which is now known as Coastguard Cottages. There were 4 houses there, and then after I was born Mum and Dad moved to 10 Church Street, the house next door to me. This is where we were brought up. Daphne went to Trimingham School, but she would not go without me. When she was about 6 years old the school closed, so we went to Overstrand School. We stayed there until we were old enough to leave. Daphne worked at Greystones, which was called Bar Haven then, at weekends and school holidays. She worked there when she left school; she served teas, ice cream etc.

Where Daphne's bungalow is, all that land was a miniature golf course so she took the money from the golfers. When the war broke out the man she worked for went to war so it was no longer a cafe, so then she went to work for Rev Page until she had to do something at 18 to help with the war. First she went to train as a nurse at Attleborough Hospital, but that was not for Daphne. She then went as a bus conductress; she did the journeys from Mundesley to Norwich. After that she went to Welwyn Garden City in a munitions factory and that is where she stayed until the war ended. She met her husband Alan, they married in 1948. Alan built their bungalow which they lived in. At night he had a tilley lamp to see with. They had a daughter, Christine, who is married to John and lives in Southrepps. Daphne did not mix in anything in the village; the bungalow was her pride and joy. If you called in to see her she always had a duster in her hand. Daphne was good to Mum and Dad, also Edwin. She looked after them and she was a marvellous cook.

2022

Alec & Margaret, Golden Wedding Day

Christmas and a Bang

I hope everyone is coping with this virus, what a terrible world to live in. It just goes on; let's hope 2022 will improve, so here's wishing everyone happiness and good health for the New Year. By the time you read this Mardle Christmas will be all over and almost forgotten about. Hope everyone made the best of it. For those like myself Christmas doesn't mean much. Years ago Christmas dinner was fantastic as it was the only time you had poultry for dinner, you never saw poultry in the Butchers, only at Christmas time. Now we have poultry all the year round, in the past it was a luxury. At this time of year during the war food was short, as it was at any time, as it was rationing but living in the country we grew our own vegetables so we were lucky. Thinking of the war years and the mines which were in the cliffs between Sidestrand and Mundesley. We would be working in the fields and there would be such a bang and when you looked up there would be a lot of soil blown in the air from that explosion. Very often if one went off it would set others off. What a waste of money, these were the highest cliffs along here and lives were lost.

Agriculture and Highways

Then I got a job with the War Agriculture. I caught a lorry near Overstrand Church, when we had picked up all the men we would go around to the farms and do what wanted to be done. There were about twenty of us. I stayed for six months. I then went to work. I started work in 1940 at Hall Farm for Mr Harrison. I was then loaned out to Mr Firman at Beacon Farm for two years. I went back to Hall Farm for a while and was then loaned out to Mr Page at Church Farm where I stayed for a while. I went back to Hall Farm and stayed there until one day the farmer said to me, "You have got to do something." I said to him, "What?" and he said, "You have got to do what I tell you." I said to him, "There is no such word as got to do, I will do what you want in a polite way". I then told him to stick his job. I went home and never went back.

I went to Mr Hicks at Bizewell Farm where I stayed for two years then to Mr Duffield at Ivy Farm, Sidestrand. I worked there for fifteen years, from working the horses, tractor driving to combining. I then thought I would have a change so I got a job with Norfolk County Council, Highways Department. I started off in construction, making new roads. I then had a lorry and had a gang of my own. We went around the villages doing what needed to be done. If there was a pot-hole or anything else that needed doing I would get a phone call. I would get it done, sometimes night time or weekends. Also winter time it would be gritting or snow ploughing, we had some bad winters then.

Cats and Pigeons

Here's wishing everyone good health, keep clear of the virus. Good luck everyone! February is halfway through; the days are now getting better with the days pulling out. Years ago, when I could do my garden, in February I would set a row of early potatoes, hoping we would get no frosts. They would be ready in June. Then as the weather got a bit warmer all the other vegetables I planted in March. I had already, November, put my sweet peas, broad beans and lettuce in. There is nothing like going in the garden and getting your own crop in.

It will be nice when it gets warmer so I can sit in the conservatory, in the sunshine, and see people go by and the traffic. At the back of the house you don't see anything, hardly a bird. First thing you see the seagulls fly in to look for land being ploughed to get the worms. I do see a lot of tame pigeons flying around from the house behind me, which is good. I was just saying to a friend, "You never see a cat in the garden nowadays." Years ago everyone had a cat, you never saw mice or rats those days as the cats would kill them, bring them home and lay them on the doorstep so you could see what they had caught. The ones our cats caught we would give to my Dad for the ferrets to eat. If a cat caught a rat it would be a healthy one so it was good ferret food. If the cat did not bring any home we would go to the farms with a torch and a stick and catch them, which was country life.

Beach Combing

Here's wishing everyone good health and keep clear of the virus. Good Luck. What a terrible mess the world is in. The News is war, what terrible pictures on the TV and in the papers with people escaping. The other day I was talking to Dot about what washed up on the beach. There were cigarettes, all sealed in tins, so they were alright. They were Players, Capstan, Gold flake, all the top makes and also tins of tobacco, which were also the top brands. A lot of wood, long planks 2ins thick, one to two foot wide and eight to ten foot long and some were longer. My Dad got a ship's mast, how he got it up the cliffs I don't know. It was used as a linen post and lasted for years.

My Uncle got a settee from the beach, after a while it got dried. It was in his house for years. Money was short then. One year near Christmas the beach was covered with boxes of oranges and grapefruits. At that time the cliffs were full of mines so you could not go down. My two young brothers walked to Mundesley to get some oranges for Mum and Dad, they had some in a bag and when they got to the top of the gangway to come home a policeman took them and said that they belonged to the Customs. Yet there was people getting boxes full. At Sidestrand a man lived in a bungalow on the cliff top, which is no longer there, had a long rope and hauled boxes up the cliff.

Time to Say Goodbye

This will be the last Mardle I do, as I am leaving Trimingham and going in a Home. My knees have given up, I cannot stand or walk without a frame and that is not easy. I have been struggling for a long while now. I am going into The Manor at Skeyton Wood. I would have left years ago it had not been for the loving care from Dot and Sue which have been marvellous to me, I cannot thank them enough. Also Sheila, Alan and Neal, Jane. I should also mention John and Les. It will be a big change in my life. I have lived in Trimingham all my life, all 95½ years, so I cannot grumble. The house I am living in I have been there 66 years. I have seen several changes over the years.

The Return of the Native

Just to let you know that I have come back to my house in Trimingham. In the end I missed my home too much. Thanks to Neal and Jane I can now again enjoy sitting in my conservatory in the sunshine. They raised the floor in the conservatory so that I can just walk into it and also put a ramp to get into the kitchen and bathroom. I would not have been able to come home without these adaptations and I cannot thank them enough. I look forward to seeing people walking by and waving at me, it makes all the difference to me. Thank you to everyone who has sent me cards and wished me well.

Mobile Dentist

Dot: One morning when I was getting Alec's breakfast there was a report on the telly about a school that had a mobile dentist in the schoolyard. Alec then said, "I can remember when I was at

Overstrand school we had a mobile dentist. It was pulled into the school yard by a horse. You had to pay for the service; if your parents could not afford the fee you did not get any treatment. Instead of an injection they used chloroform to put you to sleep to extract your teeth." It just goes to show there is nothing new and things do go round in a circle.

Alec at Home

Printed in Great Britain
by Amazon